Of course, some people are successful – clever, unusual people like Einstein, Mozart, Steven Spielberg. But this book is not for them . . .

How *badly* can people do things, if they really try?

In *The Book of Heroic Failures* you met the world's worst tourist – Mr Nicholas Scotti, the man who landed in New York and thought it was Rome. You read about the uselessness of Mr R. E. de Bruyeker, the spy who gave the enemy more information than he got from them. You read about the famous Mr Philip McCutcheon, the man with one eye and one leg who became one of the world's poorest thieves.

These are some of the greatest failures of all time, people who have been better at doing things badly than anyone else in the world. They are more than ordinary failures – they are heroes.

Now, in *More Heroic Failures*, you can read more great examples of how not to do anything right. There are the British football players who lost 21–0 to SVW Mainz of Germany. There is the great Norwegian, Mr Teigan, singer of the worst European Song Show song of 1978. And Dr Brian Richards of Deal, England, one of the unluckiest lovers there has ever been.

Stephen Pile wrote *The Book of Heroic Failures* in 1979 and said immediately, 'I will never write another book about failures.' Soon after that, he wrote *More Heroic Failures*.

Mr Pile decided never to become a writer many years ago, not long before he began wri. . . . . and wrote his first book. He lives in Ri. once tried to live outside of L. . . . . do a great many things.

The following titles are available at Levels 2, 3 and 4:

Level 2
The Birds
The Canterville Ghost and the Model
   Millionaire
Chocky
The Diary
Don't Look Behind You
Don't Look Now
Emily
Flour Babies
The Fox
The Ghost of Genny Castle
Grandad's Eleven
The Lady in the Lake
Money to Burn
Persuasion
The Railway Children
The Room in the Tower and Other
   Ghost Stories
Simply Suspense
Treasure Island
Under the Greenwood Tree
The Wave
We Are All Guilty
The Weirdo

Level 3
Black Beauty
The Black Cat and Other Stories
The Book of Heroic Failures
Calling All Monsters
A Catskill Eagle
Channel Runner
The Darling Buds of May
Dubliners
Earthdark
Forrest Gump
The Fugitive
Jane Eyre
King Solomon's Mines
Madame Doubtfire
The Man with Two Shadows and
   Other Ghost Stories

Mrs Dalloway
My Family and Other Animals
Not a Penny More, Not a Penny Less
Rain Man
The Reluctant Queen
Santorini
Sherlock Holmes and the Mystery
   of Boscombe Pool
StarGate
Summer of My German Soldier
The Thirty-nine Steps
Thunder Point
Time Bird
The Turn of the Screw
Twice Shy

Level 4
The Boys from Brazil
The Breathing Method
The Burden of Proof
The Client
The Danger
Detective Work
The Doll's House and Other Stories
Dracula
Far from the Madding Crowd
Farewell, My Lovely
Glitz
Gone with the Wind, Part 1
Gone with the Wind, Part 2
The House of Stairs
The Locked Room and Other
   Horror Stories
The Mill on the Floss
The Mosquito Coast
The Picture of Dorian Gray
Strangers on a Train
White Fang

For a complete list of the titles available in the Penguin Readers series please write to the following address for a catalogue: Penguin ELT Marketing Department, Penguin Books Ltd, 27 Wrights Lane, London W8 5TZ.

More Heroic Failures

STEPHEN PILE

Level 3

Retold by Stephen Waller and Deirdre Taylor
Series Editor: Derek Strange

PENGUIN BOOKS

PENGUIN BOOKS

Published by the Penguin Group
Penguin Books Ltd, 27 Wrights Lane, London W8 5TZ, England
Penguin Books USA Inc., 375 Hudson Street, New York, New York 10014, USA
Penguin Books Australia Ltd, Ringwood, Victoria, Australia
Penguin Books Canada Ltd, 10 Alcorn Avenue, Toronto, Ontario, Canada M4V 3B2
Penguin Books (NZ) Ltd, 182–190 Wairau Road, Auckland 10, New Zealand

Penguin Books Ltd, Registered Offices: Harmondsworth, Middlesex, England

First published by Routledge & Kegan Paul 1979
This adaptation published by Penguin Books 1995
10 9 8 7 6 5 4 3 2

Illustrations by Clive Collins

Printed in England by Clays Ltd, St Ives plc
Set in 11/13 pt Lasercomp Bembo by
Datix International Limited, Bungay, Suffolk

To the teacher:

In addition to all the language forms of Levels One and Two, which are used again at this level of the series, the main verb forms and tenses used at Level Three are:

- past continuous verbs, present perfect simple verbs, conditional clauses (using the 'first' or 'open future' conditional), question tags and further common phrasal verbs
- modal verbs: *have* (*got*) *to* and *don't have to* (to express obligation), *need to* and *needn't* (to express necessity), *could* and *was able to* (to describe past ability), *could* and *would* (in offers and polite requests for help), and *shall* (for future plans, offers and suggestions).

Also used are:

- relative pronouns: *who*, *that* and *which* (in defining clauses)
- conjunctions: *if* and *since* (for time or reason), *so that* (for purpose or result) and *while*
- indirect speech (questions)
- participle clauses.

Specific attention is paid to vocabulary development in the Vocabulary Work exercises at the end of the book. These exercises are aimed at training students to enlarge their vocabulary systematically through intelligent reading and effective use of a dictionary.

To the student:

Dictionary Words:

- When you read this book, you will find that some words are darker black than the others on the page. Look them up in your dictionary, if you do not already know them, or try to guess the meaning of the words first, without a dictionary.

Before you read:

1 Look at the words below. Put them into groups of four words about: LOVE, WORK, SPORT, WAR.

football	factory	girlfriend	enemy
husband	gun	soldiers	game
fight	marry	fishing	job
office	players	boss	kiss

2 Which words can have the same meaning?

happy	unhelpful
robber	supermarket
useless	pleased
shop	thief

3 Which words have the opposite meaning?

enemy	clever
win	boring
exciting	lose
stupid	friend

4 The stories in this book are about people who are *failures*. Can you think of ways in which these people can fail?

A man who plans to work quietly in his lunch hour.

Three men who plan to rob a post office.

Two robbers who try to escape after stealing from a shop.

A warship that shoots at an enemy ship in the Arctic Sea.

A student who dances with a girl that he likes.

A man who tries to kidnap the girl that he loves.

Now read the stories and see what really happens.

A word from Stephen Pile:

For all those writers of terrible books about how to be a **success**, I have written this book about how to be a **failure**. I think it's perfectly all right to be a failure because I am one and all my friends are, too.

INTRODUCTION

Success is not really important.

Everyone loves success. Everyone wants to do things well. But we all know that people are really good at doing things badly. Failure is the thing that we are best at. This is the difference between people and animals and we must not think that failure is bad.

Of course, *some* people are successful – clever, unusual people like Einstein, Mozart, Steven Spielberg. But this book is not for them. It is for us – people who are not very good at anything and who make a lot of mistakes.

Here in one book for the first time are the well-known names: the terrible Tito, the stupid Mountnessing robbers, the unlucky Mr Hird, and many more. They are all great failures and people have never forgotten them. They are an example to us all.

The Not Very Good Club of Great Britain

I am sure that I am not the only one who is not good at doing things. If you look at other people, you will see that most of them cannot do anything very well. Because of this fact, I think people spend too much time talking about how good they are. It is much more interesting to talk about doing things badly.

So, in 1976 I started a **club** – The Not Very Good Club of Great Britain. Anyone who belonged to my club had to be not very good at something, for example, fishing, polite conversation, trying to talk like famous people. We all met and talked about our failures. We had some wonderful evenings when people said things like: 'Yes, sheep are difficult' (a not very good painter).

In September 1976, I asked twenty of the worst failures from the club to meet for dinner at a not very good restaurant in London. The food had to wait in the oven for more than an hour while we talked about ourselves in a boring way. By the time we were ready to eat, the food was terrible.

This first dinner was a wonderful failure and so we decided to meet again one evening to play music. We all played so badly that we made a terrible noise.

After this, we decided to show people the pictures that we painted. Everyone was able to see some of the worst pictures in the world, one of which was my own

Last Supper. I always get hungry when I look at pictures of the Last Supper. So I put real food on to mine. This way other people can also enjoy the supper and have a piece of St Matthew's bread or one of St Thomas's chocolate cakes.

Many people who belong to my club have given me information for this book. But the worst failures were hard to find because people do not want to talk about these things. They don't realize that to be very bad at something you need to work hard and see things differently.

This book tells the stories of the biggest failures that we were able to find. If you are worse than this, I will be very pleased to hear from you.

The Most Unsuccessful Jump

When a show came to New York in 1978, the big question was: 'While moving at seventy-five miles an hour high above the ground, can Tito Gaona finish his jump successfully?' The short answer to this question was: 'No'.

Every night for nine months Tito tried to do his special jump with four turns sixty feet above the ground. Every night for nine months he started well, then missed his catcher and fell. But he was all right because there was something soft to fall on to. At Madison Square Gardens he was a wonderful failure, because he fell every night.

'Have you done it successfully anywhere?' someone asked him.

'Yes, once,' Tito replied. 'Before the show, when only my family was watching.'

The Most Unsuccessful Jump

The Most Unsuccessful Rubber Man

In August 1978, Janos the Rubber Man was part of a show at Southend in England. People watched him high above them with his legs uncomfortably behind his head. Slowly he came down until he was touching the ground. Then he usually turned over a few times like a ball, before standing up. The children loved it.

But one time he just sat there. 'I couldn't move,' he explained later.

One of the showmen put Janos in the back of his car and took him to hospital. Doctors took thirty minutes to straighten the Rubber Man and ordered him to lie still for a week.

The Most Unsuccessful Lunch Hour

One day in June 1978 Mr Stanley Hird was looking forward to working during his lunch hour because he had a lot of work to do. At one o'clock his wool factory outside the town of Bradford was empty and he was hoping to work better in the quiet building.

At ten past one a **cow** fell through the roof. The factory was next to a field and the cow was able to climb on to the roof from there. For thirty seconds both of them did nothing. But then the cow was angry because this was her lunch hour, too. She began to move towards Mr Hird, looking at him in a very unfriendly way with her head down. This continued for some minutes while Mr Hird carefully moved towards the door and the cow knocked boxes of wool across the floor. But then the cow, whose name was Rosie, stopped

The Most Unsuccessful Lunch Hour

to eat some green wool and Mr Hird escaped from the building. Outside, he met a farmer who was looking for a young cow. The police came and also the firemen, who needed a special lifting machine to get the animal out.

The Worst Computer

We often say that computers do things better than people. But we have forgotten the computer that the Avon local **government** bought to help them to pay their workers.

The computer's little adventure started in a small way, paying a school cleaner £75 an hour instead of 75 pence. Then it decided not to pay a kitchen worker anything for seven weeks.

Soon it started to do bigger things and paid a door-keeper £2,600 for a week's work. He sent the money back and immediately got the same again.

By this time the computer was so sure of itself that nobody could stop it. A school teacher got a year's pay every month; workers got more money than the boss; and the computer ordered some people to send more than a year's pay to the government.

In February 1975, 280 local government workers met to talk about the problem. Only eight of them had the right pay. They all decided to stop work until the local government threw away the stupid computer.

The Doctor Who Surprised a Cow

In 1977, a Dutch doctor had to go to see a sick cow. He needed to study the gases in the cow's stomach. He had to put a **tube** into the back end of the animal and light a match. But as soon as he did this, fire shot out of the tube and hit some dry grass, which started to burn. Soon all of the farm was one great fire. It cost £45,000 to build it again. The cow was all right but she was a little shaky.

The Most Useless Post Box

In 1979, workmen at Ballymacra, County Atrim in Ireland were taking down old **telegraph poles** and putting up new ones. One of the old poles had a post box on it. The workers did not have the key to unlock the metal ring that tied the post box to the pole. So they lifted the box and the metal ring over the top of the old pole and dropped it down the new one. But the new pole was thicker than the old one and so the post box did not fall all the way down. Instead, it stopped nine feet above the ground.

It stayed there for three weeks. During that time some people were able to post letters. 'I have heard,' said Mr Ernie McDermott, the postman, 'that someone left a ladder there.'

The Most Useless Post Box

The Museum That Described a Coin Wrongly

In October 1971 in County Durham some people made a big mistake. The South Shields **Museum** proudly described one of the coins on show as a Roman **coin**. Miss Fiona Gordon, who was 9 years old, told them something about the coin that surprised them. It was, in fact, a plastic coin that came from a business that sold sweet drinks. They gave them to people who returned bottles to the shop.

When they asked her to explain, she said, 'I knew because I saw the letter "R" on one side of the coin.'

A man from the museum said, 'The coin looks just like a Roman coin. We thought the letter "R" meant "Roma". In fact it was "R" for Robinsons, the business that makes the drinks.'

'The date is wrong by almost 2,000 years,' Miss Gordon said helpfully.

The Most Unsuccessful Balloon Journey

In 1823 Mr Charles Green, one of the first people to travel in a **balloon**, was getting ready for one of his balloon journeys. He climbed into the **basket** and started the fire that lifted the balloon off the ground. The balloon went up slowly but the basket stayed where it was. Someone forgot to tie the basket to the balloon or perhaps they did not tie it on purpose. Mr Green and his friend did not want to stay in the basket, so they held on to the balloon. People watched the balloon as it went over the town of Cheltenham, with Mr Green and his friend still holding on underneath it.

The Most Unsuccessful Balloon Journey

The Worst Way to Light a Fire

In 1972 Derek Langborne, from Upton, near the town of Didcot in England, put some pieces of wood into his fireplace in his living-room and began to light a fire. When the fire started, he went outside to get some more wood.

But one piece of wood wanted to warm the room very quickly and fell out of the fireplace on to the floor next to a box of smaller pieces of wood. When Mr Langborne came back, he saw that the box of wood was burning. He quickly carried it out into the garden. On the way out of the house he knocked against a jacket on the back of the door. By the time he came back, the jacket and the door were both burning.

As soon as he lifted the telephone to call the fire station in Didcot he noticed that the box of wood in the garden was standing too near his car and that his car was now burning.

He then put on his coat and ran towards his car with some water but on the way he knocked a tin of oil all over the ground.

Seeing that Mr Langborne was busy, his neighbour called the fire station. By the time the firemen arrived, Mr Langborne's coat was burning, too.

The Most Unsuccessful Man-eater

In 1970 a large, man-eating cat escaped from a show in Italy. When it saw a small boy, it naturally started to run after him. Not so naturally, the boy's mother stood in front of the animal and began to fight with it. She

The Worst Way to Light a Fire

The Most Unsuccessful Man-eater

hurt the animal's head and body so badly that it had to go to hospital.

The Most Unsuccessful Last Goodbye

In many countries, when someone dies their body lies in the church so that everyone can say a final goodbye.

The most unsuccessful final goodbye happened in March 1896 at a church in Methymni in Greece.

After two days lying in a wooden box in the church with his best clothes on, Nicephorus Glycas suddenly sat up. He looked round angrily at the people there and asked, 'What are you all looking at?'

The Most Stupid Robbers

Three thieves at Billericay in Essex spent many hours in 1971 planning to rob the post office in Mountnessing Road.

They knew the best time to do it, when there was most money in the building and no guard. They also bought guns and a car to help them escape.

So when the time came the Mountnessing robbers drove very fast through Billericay to the post office.

They jumped out of the car and ran towards the building. That was when they realized something important. The post office was not a post office now. It closed twelve years before. The building was now an ordinary shop.

Mrs Gertrude Haylock, the 76-year-old shopkeeper, later explained, 'I saw these two men running towards

The Most Stupid Robbers

the shop with guns and I said to my customer, "Here's somebody trying to be funny." '

When they got inside the shop, the robbers pointed their guns at Mrs Haylock and her customer, Mrs Constance Clarke. They told Mrs Haylock to give them all the money in the shop.

There was only £6 in the shop because there were not many customers. They took the money.

'I think they thought there were hundreds of pounds in the shop. They looked so funny dressed like robbers. It was just like in a film,' said Mrs Haylock.

After the robbers left, Mrs Clarke felt suddenly ill when she realized that they were real robbers with real guns.

The Worst Bank Robbers

In August 1975 three robbers were going through the doors of the Royal Bank of Scotland at Rothesay. The doors were the kind that went round in a circle. Suddenly the doors stopped moving when the robbers were half way through so that they could not move. Bank workers had to help them to get out. Looking uncomfortable, the robbers thanked everyone and left the building.

A few minutes later they returned and tried to rob the bank but nobody thought that they were real bank robbers. When they asked a woman for £5,000 she laughed at them. Then they tried again and asked for £500, then £50 and finally 50 pence. By this time the woman couldn't stop laughing.

Then one of the robbers jumped over the desk and fell on the floor, hurting his foot. The other two men ran to the doors but the doors caught them for a second time:

The Worst Bank Robbers

the two robbers were pushing them hard the wrong way.

The Most Unsuccessful Photograph

Mr Monte Shoemaker did something truly great in 1978. He planned to photograph an important rich man when he was doing something that people usually want to keep secret. He planned this so that the man had to pay him to keep the photograph a secret.

He hid in a bedroom cupboard. His girlfriend brought the man into the room. Mr Shoemaker waited a few minutes, then jumped out of the cupboard and photographed them. Then he asked for money.

When the photograph was ready, it did not show the rich man without his clothes on. Instead, it showed a refrigerator in the corner of the room.

The Thief Who Was Not Good At Climbing Through Windows

Our favourite sort of thief is not very quick on his feet. Mr Christopher Fleming was one of these. In 1978, Mr Fleming wanted to steal money from a Chinese restaurant in Tiverton in Devon. He planned to climb through a kitchen window and steal as much money as possible, then climb back through the window again.

In one quick unusual movement he climbed through the window and fell into a large pot of cooking oil. With the oil all over him he continued with his plan and went to where the money was.

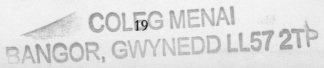

He could not find very much money, only a few coins, which he put into his pockets. Outside, the oily thief walked straight into the arms of a policeman.

The Robber Who Gave His Money Away

A man planned to steal money from a supermarket in Southampton in 1977. He went round the shop in the usual way, choosing things to buy. Then he went to pay the shopkeeper. He put £10 of coins on the desk. While the woman was counting the money he put his arm over the desk and took all the money that was there. He then ran out of the shop. But he lost £5.63 because there was only £4.37 in the desk at the time.

The woman was not sure what to do at first. She screamed for a minute and then her friend Betty came to help her.

The Most Unsuccessful Escape

One of the most unsuccessful escapes happened in Detroit in 1970. Someone stole the car that two bank robbers were planning to use to drive away from the bank. When the robbers ran out of the bank into the street, their car was gone.

But in July 1978 two robbers were much better failures than that. They were more than just unlucky – they were stupid, too. They robbed a shop in Perivale in Middlesex. When they went into the shop, they took £4,500 and then ran out to their car.

It was then that things started to get interesting. One

of the robbers, Mr O'Connor, was the driver. He jumped in, turned the key the wrong way and broke the lock. The two then jumped into another car and did the same thing again.

But that was not all. The cars were pointing the wrong way for their escape. They were pointing straight at the police station.

The Man Who Could Not Catch a Thief

During 1978 a thief returned every night to the same newspaper shop in Barking, Essex to steal £10. Every morning the money was gone and so the shopkeeper planned to catch the thief.

The shopkeeper brought a very large box into his shop. He put the box in the middle of the floor. After closing the shop at five o'clock, he climbed into the box and spent the night there.

There was no movement until fourteen hours later when the very clever detective came out of his hiding place to go to the toilet. He was away for only a few minutes. But when he returned, another £10 was gone.

The Most Unsuccessful Police Dog

In America, there was a dog, 'La Dur', who looked very frightening. He stopped working for the Orlando police in Florida in 1978 because he never did anything to worry robbers, thieves or other criminals.

The policeman whose dog it was, Rick Grim, had to

agree: 'He's useless. He just doesn't bite them. I got tired of doing the dog's work for him.'

The British examples are worse. British police taught 'Laddie' and 'Boy' to look for things that people hid. They lost their jobs after a visit to a flat in 1967.

The policeman was questioning two men, who spoke to the dogs in friendly way until the dogs went to sleep in front of the fire. When the policeman tried to take hold of the arm of one of the men, the dogs were angry and one of them bit the policeman's leg.

The Man Who Was Unhelpfully Brave

Sometimes people try to be brave to help someone in trouble. In July 1978 bank workers at Sherman Oaks in California did not want to take a packet that a man brought into the bank. They thought the man was a robber and so they sent him away with his packet. They were glad when they saw the man run outside with his packet.

Outside, another man saw the man running away from the bank and decided to try and catch him. He caught the man and carried the packet back into the bank. Inside the packet there was a smoke **bomb**, which blew all over the bank two minutes later.

It took thirty minutes for the smoke to clear.

The Most Unsuccessful Hangings

There are two hangmen that we must remember. The first of them worked in Sydney in Australia. In 1803 he tried

The Man Who Was Unhelpfully Brave

The Most Unsuccessful Hangings

three times to hang a Mr Joseph Samuels. The first two times Mr Samuels fell to the floor. The third time he just hung there until he and all the other people were tired of waiting. Since they could not hang him they decided to forgive him and he went free.

The second one was British, a Mr James Berry. Mr Berry tried three times in 1885 to hang Mr John Lee at Exeter Prison, but each time he was unable to open the special door under the prisoner's feet.

After this, the British government decided to send Lee to prison for a long time instead. He came out of prison in 1917, travelled to Australia and lived there until 1933.

The Worst Fisherman

Thomas Birch was a man of learning who lived in the 1700s. He liked to go fishing but he didn't catch very many fish. So he decided to dress like a tree to hide himself from the fish. He made some clothes that were like a tree, with little holes for his eyes.

He put on the clothes and went down to the river. But he still did not catch anything. No fish came near him. But dogs came to see him and friends sat down next to him to have their lunch.

The Worst Game of Football

In 1973 the Oxbarn football players were getting ready to play a game in Germany. The players were a group of friends who usually played on Sundays against other

The Worst Fisherman

small local clubs in Britain. They were looking forward to the game and also a holiday in Germany.

When they walked out into the very large football ground in Germany, they realized that they were playing one of the best German clubs – S V W Mainz. The German footballers thought the British players belonged to another club – Wolverhampton Wanderers – which was one of the strongest football clubs in Britain at that time.

An Oxbarn player said, 'I thought it was a bit strange when I saw the size of the crowd.'

About half way through the game – it was already 15–0 to the Germans – the crowd saw Oxbarn's centre fall to his knees. He looked like he was crying. Naturally, the German crowd were very pleased that the Oxbarn club was playing instead of Wolverhampton Wanderers.

'They were very good about it,' one of the Oxbarn players said. 'When we got the ball, they started to shout to help us win.'

Oxbarn Football Club lost 21–0.

The Smallest Football Crowd

Who remembers that great game between Leicester City and Stockport County on 7 May 1921? It is famous for having the smallest crowd. Only thirteen people watched it. In fact both sides were playing away from home. Stockport's home ground was closed and so they had to play in the very large ground belonging to the well-known club Manchester United.

The Happy Failure

A Norwegian singer was singing a wonderfully boring song in the European Song Show in 1978. Many singers from different countries were there. At the end of the show people from each country had to decide which song was the best. They also decided which song was the worst. Unusually they all agreed: 'Norway gets zero out of ten.'

Next morning the newspaper stories were naturally all about the Norwegian singer, Mr Teigan, while there were only a few words about the winning singer, Izhar Cohen. After the show newspaper photographers crowded round Mr Teigan, welcoming him like a popstar.

'This is my greatest success,' he said. 'I have done something that nobody has done before me. I'm the first Norwegian to get zero. After the show they asked me to sing parts of the song sixty times for the photographers. And I'm going to be on television and singing all over Europe. People have never been so interested in me before.'

The Funniest Modern Pictures

To understand modern pictures, you have to be able to think in a free way about them. Nothing has shown this more than a Frankfurt show of works by an exciting new painter, Yamasaki, in 1978. The man who was showing the pictures, Mr Feddersen, wrote about Yamasaki's wonderfully bright colours and strong, interesting shapes. In only three hours, visitors bought all twenty-two of the pictures for as much as £500 each.

The Funniest Modern Pictures

Excitement grew when the news came that the painter was there and was ready to answer questions about his work. You can guess how glad all the free-thinking people were when Mr Feddersen brought in a **monkey**. 'He just threw paint all over the place,' he explained.

He wanted the money for a different kind of show in which animals did funny things for children to watch.

The Most Unsuccessful Showing of a Picture

Between 17 October and 3 December 1961 the famous picture *Le Bateau* by Henri Matisse hung in a show in New York. But the great painter's work was hanging the wrong way – the top was at the bottom. The picture shows a sailing boat in the water on a summer's day. About 116,000 visitors went round the show before the painter's son noticed the mistake.

The Most Unsuccessful Warship

In times of war, everyone must be ready to die for his country. Nothing has shown this more clearly than the warship *HMS Trinidad* in 1941 when it used an underwater **weapon** against a German ship. The two ships were sailing in the Arctic Sea and the icy water changed the way the weapon travelled. Instead of going straight towards the German ship it began to turn. In a few seconds the weapon turned round and was on its way back to the *Trinidad*. The sailors successfully hit a ship but sadly it was theirs. The *Trinidad* could not sail again for the rest of the war.

The Weapon That Was Too Secret

In the Franco-Prussian War, the French side had a very secret weapon. The 'Mitrailleuse' machine gun was the first of its kind and they thought it was sure to kill many enemy soldiers.

They decided to keep the new weapon secret until the first day of the war in 1870. But by that time the French soldiers were too busy to learn how to use it.

The Most Unsuccessful Study of a Weapon

German soldiers went into the town of Brest in France in 1940 and found a new French secret weapon, the 15-inch 'Richelieu' gun. They were very pleased and they immediately asked someone to study the new weapon. They wanted to know how to use it and they wanted to know quickly. But the man who was studying the weapon did not like working fast. He was always careful and he wrote down every little thing about the weapon. He did not finish the study until April 1944. Also, it was not possible to use the gun for the rest of the war because there were no more bullets left for it. The man used all of them during the study.

The Most Useless Weapon

The most useless weapon is perhaps the Russian one which used dogs. In the Second World War they taught dogs to think about food every time they saw a **tank**. So when the dog saw a tank, it ran under it to look for

The Most Useless Weapon

food. The idea was to tie bombs to the dogs, to kill the soldiers in the enemy tanks.

But the dogs ran only to Russian tanks and many of the Russians had to turn back. They very soon stopped using dog-bombs.

The Worst Man-to-Man Fight

In 1645 there was a fight between Sir Hierome Sankey and Sir William Petty and people remembered it for many years. It happened in London – nobody knows what the fight was about.

Sir Hierome was a frightening man. Sir William did not really want to fight him.

Sir William was the one who chose the place and the weapons for the fight. He had a very clever idea. He chose a very dark room so that they could not see and weapons that were too heavy to lift.

This was the worst fight until December 1971, when two Uruguayan soldiers could not agree. It happened after one of them called the other a name that he did not like.

They decided to meet in a local park and to fight with guns. Standing with seventy-five feet between them, they both shot thirty-seven bullets. But neither of them hit the other man.

Later, a friend of one of the soldiers explained this surprising fact. They both forgot to put on their glasses before the fight.

The Worst Local Government Worker

Señor José Ramon del Cuet once had an important job in the local government of Coacaloco in Mexico. In June 1978 he left his job because he felt that he was not a success. Four thousand local people helped him to decide to do this. They all went to the local government offices and ordered him to eat twenty-five kilos of bananas and he did. Then they told him to leave his job immediately.

The Most Unsuccessful Fight Against the Government

In 1964 enemies of the Italian government were planning to take over the government in Rome. They ordered their men to meet outside the city. Luckily, most of them did not know Rome very well and got lost in the small streets on the way to the city centre.

The government did not hear about the plan until five years later, when they immediately tried to get more information about it.

In 1974 there was another plan of the same kind in the south of Italy that was a failure, too. This time it was not because they got lost. One of them explained, 'It was raining too hard.'

The Most Unsuccessful Dancer

In 1977 ambulance men carried Signor Paco Vila, a student from Palermo in Italy, out of a night club because a girl touched him.

The Most Unsuccessful Dancer

'I love big English women,' he said when he woke up in a hospital bed. 'But they laugh at me because I am not heavy enough.'

He was really quite thin and he bravely decided to do something about this. He started to wear thick pullovers under his shirt.

That night at the club he dressed himself well and a girl wanted to dance with him. She was an English girl on holiday in Palermo.

During one of his faster dances he got very tired. When the girl touched him, he fell to the floor. Later, in hospital, doctors found seventeen pullovers under his shirt.

The Most Unsuccessful Lovers

One day in 1976 Dr Brian Richards of Deal in Kent was in Regent's Park in London. He saw a man, with very few clothes on, enjoying himself in the back of a sports car with his girlfriend. Suddenly the man hurt his back.

Because the man hurt himself badly and could not move, his girlfiend was unable to get out of the car and ask for help. So she screamed.

Dr Richards, an ambulance man, a fireman and a large crowd of other people heard her screams. They all stood in a circle round the car. 'You'll never get them out of there,' said the fireman and started cutting the back off the car.

During this time, two women served tea through the car window.

In the end they carried the lover to hospital. Ambu-lance men told the girlfriend not to worry. 'I'm not worried about him,' she answered. 'How am I going to explain to my husband? It was his car.'

The Most Unsuccessful Kidnap

In August 1972 Mr Darsun Yilmaz of Damali on the Black Sea was in love with his neighbour's daughter but she did not want to marry him. So he decided to kidnap her. Soon after midnight the brave Yilmaz arrived in her garden with a ladder. When he went into her room, he threw a coat over her head and carried her down to the car. While he did this, he spoke words of love softly into the end of the coat that was probably nearest her ear.

They drove away into the night, happiness in their hearts and stars in the sky. But when he opened the coat and held out his lips for a kiss, he saw to his great surprise that it was the girl's 91-year-old grandmother. She was glad to hit him as hard as she could.

The Man Who Was Never Able to Ask his Lover to Marry Him

In the late 1800s a teacher in London was in love with a rich young woman, Gwendolin, who lived in Sussex. One weekend he went to the family's large old home near Lewes, to ask her to marry him. On his first night there, he woke up at 3a.m. wanting a glass of water. Trying to find the bathroom in the dark house, he knocked something over. Next morning he woke up to see that there was paint all over a beautiful old chair, a favourite chair of Gwendolin's mother. He left immediately without seeing the woman that he loved.

Later, when everything was all right with Gwendolin again, he went back to try again. This time he decided to stay only half an hour in the afternoon to be sure that something terrible did not happen. He met Gwendolin's mother and asked to see her daughter. While the mother was out of the room he sat down on a soft, warm chair. In fact, he sat on the family dog, a little Pekinese. Sadly the dog died. He left again without seeing Gwendolin. He never married her.

EXERCISES

Vocabulary Work

Look back at the 'Dictionary Words' in this book. Write sentences to show what each of the words means. Use *two or more* words in each sentence.

success	club	government
cow	tube	museum
coin	telegraph poles	balloon
basket	hanging	monkey
bomb	weapon	tank

Comprehension

1 Read 'The Museum That Described a Coin Wrongly' again. Now read these sentences and write 'T' for the ones that are true.

  a The coin was made of plastic.

  b Miss Gordon knew the coin was not a Roman coin because she saw the letter 'R' on one side of it.

  c The letter 'R' was the last letter of the name of a business that sold sweet drinks.

  d The museum did not believe what Miss Gordon said about the coin.

2 Here are parts of sentences about four of the stories. Can you put the sentences together?

  a Oxbarn football players   fell into a large pot of cooking oil.

  b A cow   stayed on the ground.

  c The balloon basket   flew to Germany.

  d The thief   fell through the roof.

Which stories are the sentences about?

3 Read 'The Funniest Modern Pictures' again. Now choose the right answers.

  a The visitors bought the pictures because:
    i) they were only £500 each.
    ii) they thought they were exciting.

  b The painter:
    i) was a monkey.
    ii) was not ready to answer questions about his work.

  c Mr Feddersen:
    i) showed the wrong pictures.
    ii) showed the pictures because he wanted to sell them.

4 In which stories do we read about these things? Why are they important?
  a a Pekinese dog   c a computer
  b telegraph poles   d some pullovers

5 In which stories do these things happen?
  a A thief gives money to a supermarket.
  b A woman in a bank starts laughing at some bank robbers.
  c A singer sings a very, very boring song.
  d A police dog bites a policeman's leg.
  e Four thousand people order a man to eat a lot of bananas.
  f A man takes a photo of a refrigerator.
  g Some English football players play a game in Germany.
  h A thief falls into a large pot of cooking oil.

Discussion

1 Who do you think is the worst failure in this book. Why?
2 'Success is not really important.' Do you agree? Why or why not?

Writing

Write a letter to The Not Very Good Club of Great Britain, telling them about something that you are not very good at (100–150 words).